Diving into Finance

I0407105

A Teen's Guide to Money Management

To my friends, family, and teachers who have taught me so much. I am very grateful.

Table of Contents

Introduction

Learning about money management and finances is not only exciting but also a very useful skill! Learning how to make smart financial decisions while young will set you apart from your peers and make your life a lot easier. In this book, you will learn about concepts like saving, investing, money management, goal setting, and making money. After reading this book you will have a greater understanding of personal finance and advance above your peers and impress others with your knowledge! It's never too early to start learning such a valuable skill as money management.

Chapter 1:
Why Care?

Why Should I Care and/or Learn About Finance?

Being a teen, it can feel like financial planning and finances are a future problem. It may seem like you don't have to worry about finances right now. Despite this, there are many reasons to learn about finance at a young age.

Money is Everywhere

In life, there is hardly any situation where you won't use money. Having a strong foundation of financial literacy will never go to waste. To do almost anything you need to understand how money works and be prepared to make financial decisions.

A Lifetime of Financial Independence

As a teen, there are a lot of financial decisions that influence the rest of your life. The decision to or not to go to college, buying and paying for a car, savings, credit cards, and emergency funds are all things that are important to get a head start on. By making poor financial decisions at a young age, you could be stuck in debt as an adult. On the other hand, by making smart financial decisions now, you can start on the right food as an adult and have a lifetime of financial freedom.

Benefits of Compounding

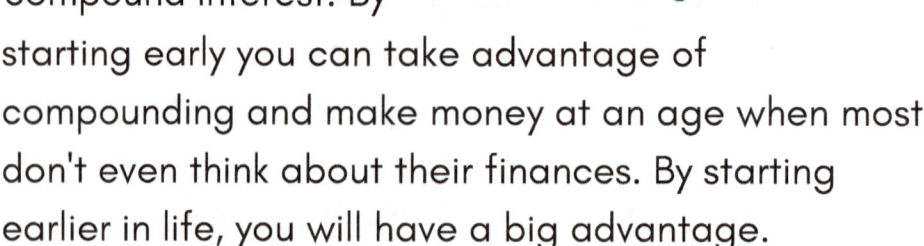

You'll learn later about compound interest. By starting early you can take advantage of compounding and make money at an age when most don't even think about their finances. By starting earlier in life, you will have a big advantage.

Financial Literacy Can Help Reduce Anxiety

Many adults find the topic of finances stressful. By understanding how finances work and being financially literate at a young age, you can reduce future anxiety about money.

Setting the Tone for Financial Success

By learning about finances young, and practicing and reinforcing wise financial habits, you can set a positive tone for your financial future. It's easier to learn things and create habits when you're young. If you practice smart spending and financial habits now, you will most likely carry those into your adult life.

FUTURE

You Have A Parent/Guardian Close By to Help You

When you are a teen, chances are that you don't have to worry about paying for big expenses (like a house or other basic needs). This gives you  more freedom to try new things. Along with this, your parent or guardian is close to answer questions and offer advice, that might be difficult to ask for as you get older.

Overall, money is an important topic that is applied everywhere. By starting young, there are many great opportunities that will benefit your future.

Chapter 2

Goal Setting

"A goal without a plan is just a wish." -Antoine de Saint-Exupery

Why should I set goals?

Goal setting (and achieving) is one of the most important parts of not only managing money but doing anything in life. Lots of times goals aren't achieved because the goal itself isn't very clear. If you don't even know what you are trying to do, how are you supposed to do it? That's why it's important to set SMART goals.

Goals

S is for **Specific**

M is for **Measurable**

A is for **Attainable**

R is for **Realistic**

T is for **Time-Bound**

Specific

A goal should use actual numbers and be precise. Don't just say 'I'll make more money', say 'I'll make $5'. The second goal is more specific and you'll be able to tell if you achieved what you wanted to. With the first goal, even if you only made a penny, you still would have technically achieved it, but realistically that's not what you wanted or meant.

Measurable

A goal should also be trackable. Similar to a goal being specific, you want to be able to tell if you actually completed your goal. You should be able to track and measure what you have done and what you need to do (this concept makes more sense when you have read the other parts of goal setting).

Attainable

A goal should be possible. 99% of the time it would be impossible for a person to make $100,000,000,000 in 3 days. Goals should be challenging, but not impossible. Make sure your goal is actually attainable.

Realistic

Set goals that are realistic for YOU. When creating a goal, take into account personal things that might affect your ability to achieve the goal. Be honest with yourself and know what you're actually capable of. For example, if your goal was to make $500 in the next 2 weeks by walking dogs, but for the next month you are bedridden because of an injury, that goal wouldn't be realistic.

Time-Bound

It's important to set deadlines for goals. For example, if you say 'I want to make $500', that goal is not time-bound. If you made that goal when you are 13 and by the time you are 25 you have $500 more than you did when you were 13, you would have technically completed the goal, but that probably wasn't what you meant when creating the goal when you were 13. This goes hand-in-hand with the first 2 aspects of a goal (being specific and measurable). By adding the element of time the goal becomes more specific and much easier to measure.

Not SMART Goal: "I will make lots of money soon."

SMART Goal: "I will make $500 in the next month by mowing lawns."

The $500 is a specific amount that is easy to measure. In a month you could easily tell if you made $500 or not.

The next month is a clear time. If you're writing a goal it's best to put an exact date (like March 1st, for example. Unlike the first example, you have clearly stated when you want to make $500. Soon could be within the next 5 days or the next 5 months, were as a month is very clear.

To be even more specific in your goal it's best to put in a plan of action. Mowing lawns clearly states how the person writing the goal intends on making $500.

10

What Are Some of Your Financial Goals?

It's always better to plan and to set goals in advance, so think about your future. What are some things you want or will want (or need) soon? Will you be driving soon? Maybe you need to start saving for a car. What about college? Do you plan on going? It's never too early to start saving. Even start saving for retirement, it couldn't hurt. Think about some financial goals that you might have for your future.

What are you saving for?

Chapter Review & Questions

- SMART stands for Specific, Measurable, Attainable, realistic, and Time-Bound.
- SMART goals are very clear and set clear expectations.

- What are some of your personal goals?
- Have you ever made a goal and achieved it? If so, why do you think this happened?
- Have you ever made a goal and not achieved it? If so, why do you think this happened?
- Do you think you'll be driving in the near future? Are you driving now? Do you want to buy a car?
- Are you planning on going to college? Have you started saving?

Use the space below to practice writing out a SMART Goal that you have. I encourage you to grab a separate piece of paper and create a financial goal for yourself, and actually go and achieve it. You don't have to do anything big or crazy, it could be as simple as adding $25 dollars to your savings after a certain amount of time.

Chapter 3:
Savings

A big part of finances is saving. You probably are already saving your money in some way. For instance, you might keep your coins in a piggy bank, in a shoe box under your bed, or even in a savings account at a bank.

Why should I save my money?

It's important to have some savings. If an emergency were to happen and you needed cash, having savings would allow you to pay without going into debt. If you see an item that you want, you could buy it using the money you saved, and not have to wait until you made money to buy that item.

Emergency Funds

An emergency fund is money that you have saved specifically for emergencies ONLY. It's a good idea to save about $300–$500 and to only spend that in case of an emergency.

If you would like to buy something, you don't need to go into debt to buy it. For example, if you want to go to the movies with your friends and it cost $5 for a movie ticket, you could just use the money you already have saved up. If you didn't have money saved, you would have to ask your parents to borrow $5. Then you would have the stress of having to make money to pay them back. Even then, your parents may not let you borrow $5, and you would have to pass up seeing a movie with your friends.

Spending: Needs vs. Wants

Learning to control your spending is a huge part of savings. In order to control your spending, you first need to understand your needs vs. wants. Needs are something that you need. They aren't limited to the basic needs of survival (like food and water) but are things that life would be difficult without in general. For example, when you get older you might need a car to get to work and school. Or you might need a laptop for school or work. Wants are things that you don't need and that you only (or mostly) get for pure pleasure. A want might be to go see a movie with friends or get a fancy gadget that all your peers have. A want could also be a car (even though A little bit ago I said that a car might be a need).

For want vs. need, it sometimes depends on the type of thing that you are buying. For example, you may need a car but you want a fancy $60,000 car, when you only need a simple $25,000 car. See the difference? Same with a pair of shoes. Almost any cheap pair of shoes you buy at the store will work to protect your feet and provide comfort, but you still might want a pair of trendy $150 shoes.

Here are some examples of Needs vs. Wants:

Needs	Wants
• A Car • A Laptop • Shoes • Food	• A High-End Mercedes • MacBook Air • A Pair of Air Jordans • Eating Out at an Expensive Restaurant with Friends

Spending: Needs vs. Wants Continued

This doesn't mean that you can only buy the bare minimum and you can't buy a nice pair of shoes. It just means you have to be aware of the difference between wants and needs. If there is a high-end item that you want it's fine to buy it, just make sure it's something that you actually want and you put time and effort into considering buying it (in other words, avoid just impulse buying). Along with that, it never hurts to look on the internet for sales and coupons which could lower the price of an item. One thing to remember when buying these wants is to try to always pay with money you already have (don't go into debt).

For example: If you want a nice pair of $150 shoes, save up for those shoes then buy them. Don't get a loan from your parents or put them on a credit card (if you have one). If you put the expense on a credit card the debt will collect interest as time goes on, and that nice pair of shoes could end up costing you way more than $150. If you were to take a loan from your parents you would be chained to that debt and before you could purchase anything else you would have to pay them back first causing you lots of stress.

Where do I keep my savings?

Keeping your money in your bedroom in a special spot, definitely works, but it is not always the best way to save your money.

Savings Accounts

Savings accounts at banks is a great way to keep your money safe. A savings account is similar to a piggy bank. You deposit your money and your money will sit there and stay safe. Often savings accounts will give you some interest, but typically it's a very small amount. With a savings account, you can withdraw money relatively easily (assuming you don't withdraw below the minimum balance) and deposit money whenever. Because your money is stored at a bank, you won't have the temptation to use it.

For example, if you see something you want to buy, it's slightly more difficult to withdraw money from a savings account, than it is to just pull money out of a piggy bank in your bedroom. With a savings account you also won't be able to swipe a debit card (that's connected to your savings account) so again, you are less likely to spend your savings. You will need your parent's help setting up a savings account, but it is definitely an easy way to save your money.

No Amount Too Small

When saving it's important to save as much as you can, even small amounts of money. If you find a quarter on the ground, put it in your piggy bank (even though it seems small, it can add up quickly). When buying things, look at different stores or websites, and see which one offers the best price for the item you want. Don't disregard the small savings. In the long run, those small searches can save you a lot!

Here are some ways to save:
-Visit coupon websites
-Visit brand websites
-Download browser extensions
-Look in the mail for offers
-Download cash-back apps

Chapter Review & Questions

- Savings can help you pay for items in the future without going into debt
- It's helpful and important to have an emergency fund with $300-$500
- Make sure to pay with your own money for wants
- It's okay to treat yourself to wants sometimes, just don't impulse buy
- While piggy banks work, a savings account can be helpful, and take your money management skills to the next level
- Save money whenever possible. Look for coupons, and sales, and compare prices at different stores and websites.

- Do you have any savings?
- Do you have an emergency fund? If so, how much is in it?
- What are some of your wants?
- What are some things you need, or will need in the near future?
- Do you have a savings account or want to open one?
- Do you compare prices and save even small amounts of money?

Chapter 4:
Budgeting

A budget is a plan for how you will spend your money. Budgeting is a good habit for anyone to get into. Budgets can help you save money for future expenses and goals. It can help you avoid going into debt and reduce stress about bills or other expenses.

How to Create My Own Budget

To start off, you will want to write down a list of what you currently spend your money on. It's helpful to monitor your expenses on a piece of paper, that way you can see exactly how much money you spend on each thing.

Next, you should categorize your expenses. For example, if you notice that in the last month you went out to dinner, saw a movie with friends, and went to an amusement park, you might create a category for entertainment.

In your budget, you will want to write down any fixed expenses. A fixed expense is an expense where you pay the same amount every month for the same thing. For example, if you pay your phone bill, that might be $20 every month. No matter how much you call or don't call that number will be the same. Other expenses that change from month to month are variable expenses.

Fixed
- Phone bill

Variable
- Clothes
- Going out
- Toys
- Gifts
- Random

You also need to figure out how much money you make each month. If your income varies a lot from month to month then you can slightly alter your budget to account for this.

First, make a chart of your fixed expense(s) (if you have any) and how much each expense cost you every month.

Fixed Expenses	Monthly Income: $100
• Phone Bill	$20
Total:	$20

If Your Income is Relatively Consistent Each Month:

Write down the rest of your expenses, and allocate however much money you need for the expenses each month. Make sure the total you spend on both variable and fixed expenses does not exceed your monthly income.

Fixed Expenses   **Monthly Income: $100**
- Phone Bill $20

_____

Total Fixed Expenses: $20

_____

Variable Expenses
- Entertainment $30
- Clothes $25
- Toys $15
- Savings $10

_____

Total Variable Expenses: $80

Fixed Expenses + Variable Expenses = Monthly Income
$20 + $80 = $100 ✓

If Your Income Varies Each Month

Write down your variable expenses that are needs. For example, if you were living on your own, food would be a necessity. If your parents pay for all your variable expenses that are needs then you can skip this step.

Write down all your wants and allocate a percentage of income to go to these wants. For example, you could say that 25% of your monthly income (after paying for fixed expenses) went to entertainment. Then if one month you make $20 (after paying for your fixed expenses), you would have $5 for entertainment. But if the next month you make $100, you would have $25 for entertainment. See how the amount changes based on your monthly income.

Month A Income: $100
Month B Income: $200

Fixed Expenses
- **Phone Bill** $20

Total Fixed Expenses: $20

Variable Expenses
- **Food (need)** $50
- **Clothes**   30%
- **Toys**   15%
- **Savings**   20%
- **Entertainment**   35%

Month's Income - Fixed Expenses - Variable Need(s) = Amount to Spend on Variable Want(s)

$20 + $80 = $100 ✓

Month A Income: $100   Month B Income: $200

Fixed Expenses		Month A	Month B
• Phone Bill	$20	⟶	
Total Fixed Expenses:	$20		

Variable Expenses

		Month A	Month B
• Food (need)	$50	⟶	
• Clothes	30%	$9	$39
• Toys	15%	$4.5	$19.5
• Savings	20%	$6	$26
• Entertainment	35%	$10.5	$45.5

Month's Income - Fixed Expenses - Variable Need(s) =
Amount to Spend on Variable Want(s)

Month A: $100 - $20 - $50 = $30
Month B: $200 - $20 - $50 = $130

Month A

Clothes: $30 x 30% = $9
Toys: $30 x 15% = $4.5
Savings: $30 x 20% = $6
Entertainment: $30 x 35%
= $10.5

Month B

Clothes: $130 x 30% =$39
Toys: $130 x 15% = $19.5
Savings: $130 x 20% = $26
Entertainment: $130 x
35% = $45.5

As you can see this method is more complicated, but it works for people who don't have to pay for their needs, and just want to figure out around how much money they should spend on different expenses each month. **Important Note:** I highly recommend creating a category in your budget to put towards savings.

- A budget is a plan for how you spend your money.
- Budgets can help you save for future expenses.
- Budgets can reduce the stress of not knowing how you will be able for something.
- Budgets can help prevent you from going into debt.
- To create a budget you need to figure out your income, fixed expenses, and variable expenses.

- What are some of your variable expenses?
- What are some of your fixed expenses?
- Do you make the same amount of money each month?
- Have you ever created a budget before?
- Do you have to pay for any of your needs?

Chapter 5:
Credit

Credit is a way to buy things now and pay for them later. This is based on people's willingness and trust to pay bills.

Pros of Credit

- Current use of goods and services; You can use something now, without having to pay for it now
- Allows purchases even if you can't afford to pay for it
- Can help pay for financial emergencies
- Easier to return items
- More convenient than cash or check
- Provides a record of expenses
- Safer than carrying cash

Cons of Credit

- The temptation to spend money you do not have
- Can create long-term financial problems
- Credit cost money; you might end up paying lots of interest
- Ties up future income

Types of Credit

There are two types of credit: **Closed-End Credit** and **Open-End Credit**

Closed-End Credits are one-time loans for a specific amount of money. Think of a car loan, it's a one-time loan only for the amount of money a car costs (you couldn't go buy a burger and put it on your car loan).

Open-End Credits are lines of credit that you can use whenever needed until the credit max is reached (the limit to how much money you can spend). An example would be a credit card. If you wanted you could buy a burger, then a flower, and then a stuffed animal (or any assortment of random items) and put it on your card.

Credit Score

If you walk into a bank and ask for a loan, how do they know you will repay the loan? How do they know that you are trustworthy? A credit score (sometimes known as a FICO score) is a number that determines your creditworthiness (how likely you are to repay a loan). A credit score is a number between 300 to 850. The higher the score, the better. A high credit score tells lenders that you are likely to pay back a loan. 3 main companies keep track of your credit score: Equifax, Experian, and TransUnion. These credit bureaus will send you your credit report if you ask for it.

What Determines Your Credit Score?

Types of Credit Used (10%): If you can handle a variety of different lines of credit at once, it shows lenders that you can successfully manage many financial obligations which is a good thing, which could improve your credit score!

New Credit (10%): Did you just open lots of new lines of credit at once? If so, this can harm your credit score. It can be seen as risky to open lots of lines of credit in a short amount of time.

Length of Credit History (15%): Have you managed your credit well for a long time? If so, this will help boost your credit score! Since you're young, you most likely haven't used credit for a while (or at all) which is fine, because it just takes time!

Payment History (35%): Do you pay back your debts on time? If you do great! By making sure you pay your payments on time you can improve your credit score.

Amounts Owed (Capacity)(30%): Do you have a lot of debts you haven't paid back? This could harm your credit score. It's important to make sure you don't owe a lot in debt to others, for the sake of your credit score.

Is Credit Right for You?

Should you get a credit card? The 5 C's of credit are 5 different ways to evaluate if you are in a good position to use credit.

5 C's of Credit

Character: Will you repay the loan? Are you a responsible person who will repay a loan? Character looks at your character. If you are not a responsible person, credit might be problematic for you.

Capacity: Can you repay the loan? Even if you are responsible, are you financially able to repay the loan? If not, you probably want to reconsider the purchase.

Capital: What is your net worth and what are your assets?

Collateral: What if you can't repay the loan? If you can't repay the loan what could you sell to help pay back the loan? Do you have lots of savings? An expensive painting? A house?

Condition: What if your job is insecure? What are your financial conditions like right now? If your job is insecure, this might not be the best time to take out a loan.

Credit can be a very helpful tool as long as you are responsible and able to pay for what you buy. Typically if you don't have a high credit score interest rates will be higher. Meaning, that if you miss a payment, it can be very expensive. No matter what your interest rate is, credit can get out of control fast. It's very important you pay your payments on time and in full.

Note: If you have never used credit before, your credit score is not 0, you just don't have a credit score.

Loan Sharks

Be careful of Loan Sharks. Loan Sharks are people or entities who will give you poor loans with high-interest rates. If you have a low credit score, most reliable lenders, won't give you a loan. If they do, that might signal that they are not reliable. Often when things seem good to be true, it's because they are not true.

Make sure when you get your first credit card or loan that you are responsible and can make the payments. Talk to your parents or a trusted adult to get their advice when you think you might want a credit card.

Tip

A great way to help boost your credit score when you are young is to get a gas card. This card would only be used to buy gas (so you won't be tempted to buy more things that you can't afford).

Chapter Review & Questions

- Credit is a way to buy things now and pay for them later
- Consider the 5 C's of credit (Character, Capacity, Collateral, Conditions, and capital) before opening a line of credit
- It's important to have a good credit score
- Length of Credit History, New Credit, Payment History, Amount Owed, and Types of Credit are all factors that determine a credit score

- Have you used credit before?
- Do your parents have a credit card?
- Do you think you're responsible enough to use credit? If not, that's completely fine, most people choose not to use credit until they are older.

Chapter 6

Interest

At first, interest might seem a bit complicated or confusing, but after a little bit, it will start to make a lot more sense.

What is Interest?

Interest is how much a borrower pays to take out a loan, and the money a lender receives. A borrower is a person, company, bank, or entity that takes out a loan from another person, company, bank, or entity (the lender). The principle is how much the borrower borrows from the lender. Debt is the state of owing money to another person or entity. For example, a borrower would be in debt to a lender.

Simple Interest

Simple interest is where interest stays the same throughout the time of a loan. With simple interest, the interest is a percentage of the principal and will continue to be that amount, never changing.

An Example:

John goes to his friend Sally and asks for $10 as a loan. Sally agrees to give him $10, but she says that every week John hasn't paid her back, he will pay her 10% simple interest. 10% of $10 is $1. So every week that John hasn't paid Sally back her full $10, he will also be paying her an extra $1 in interest. Let's say that John pays Sally $3 a week for the loan. $1 of this $3 would go to the interest payment, so John is only paying back $2 of his principal each week. Here is a graph showing the situation:

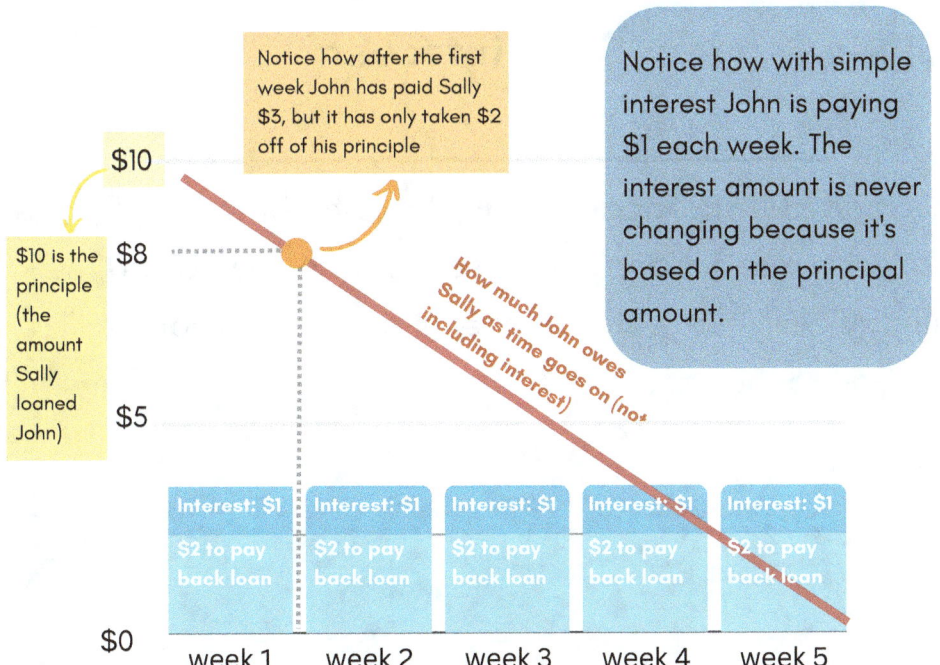

Notice how after the first week John has paid Sally $3, but it has only taken $2 off of his principle

Notice how with simple interest John is paying $1 each week. The interest amount is never changing because it's based on the principal amount.

$10

$10 is the principle (the amount Sally loaned John)

$8

$5

How much John owes Sally as time goes on (not including interest)

Interest: $1   Interest: $1   Interest: $1   Interest: $1   Interest: $1

$2 to pay back loan $2 to pay back loan $2 to pay back loan $2 to pay back loan $2 to pay back loan

$0   week 1   week 2   week 3   week 4   week 5

To calculate simple interest the equation is simple:

Principle x **Interest** x **Period**

How much the borrower borrows from the lender

The cost to borrow money (typically a percentage or decimal)

The time that the borrower borrows money

Here's the equation with the John and Sally example:

$10 x 10% (or 0.10) x 5 weeks
$1 x 5 weeks = $5 in interest

This means that because Sally let John borrow $10, she will make $5 and because John borrowed $10, he will pay Sally $5. In total (over the 5 weeks) John will pay Sally $15.

Compound Interest

Compound interest is essentially interest on interest. If you earn interest every year, then at the end of the year the interest will be added to your principal amount. This means the following year you will not only earn interest on the principal amount but also the interest earned from the previous year(s). This means the interest is not the same amount each time you earn interest.

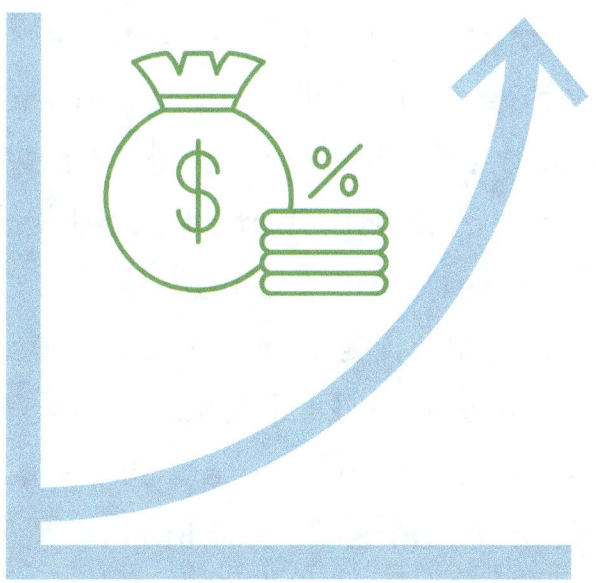

An Example:

Let's say Jill opens up a savings account at her local bank. Jill puts $100 into her savings account and never adds more money into the account (so the principal is $100). The bank tells Jill that she will make 10% interest which is compounded yearly (side note: A 10% interest rate on a savings account is very high and you are unlikely to make that much interest. The numbers are used for simplicity of math purposes only). After 1 year of Jill's money being in a savings account, she makes $10 in interest. That money is put back into her savings account, so now her account balance is $110. After the 2nd year, Jill still gets 10% interest, but now it's 10% of the $110. So after the 2nd year, Jill makes $11 in interest. That $11 is added back into the savings account, so now her account balance is $121. This process continues, so by the 3rd year Jill will make $12.10 in interest. As you can see the amount of interest Jill makes increases each year, because it's being compounded.

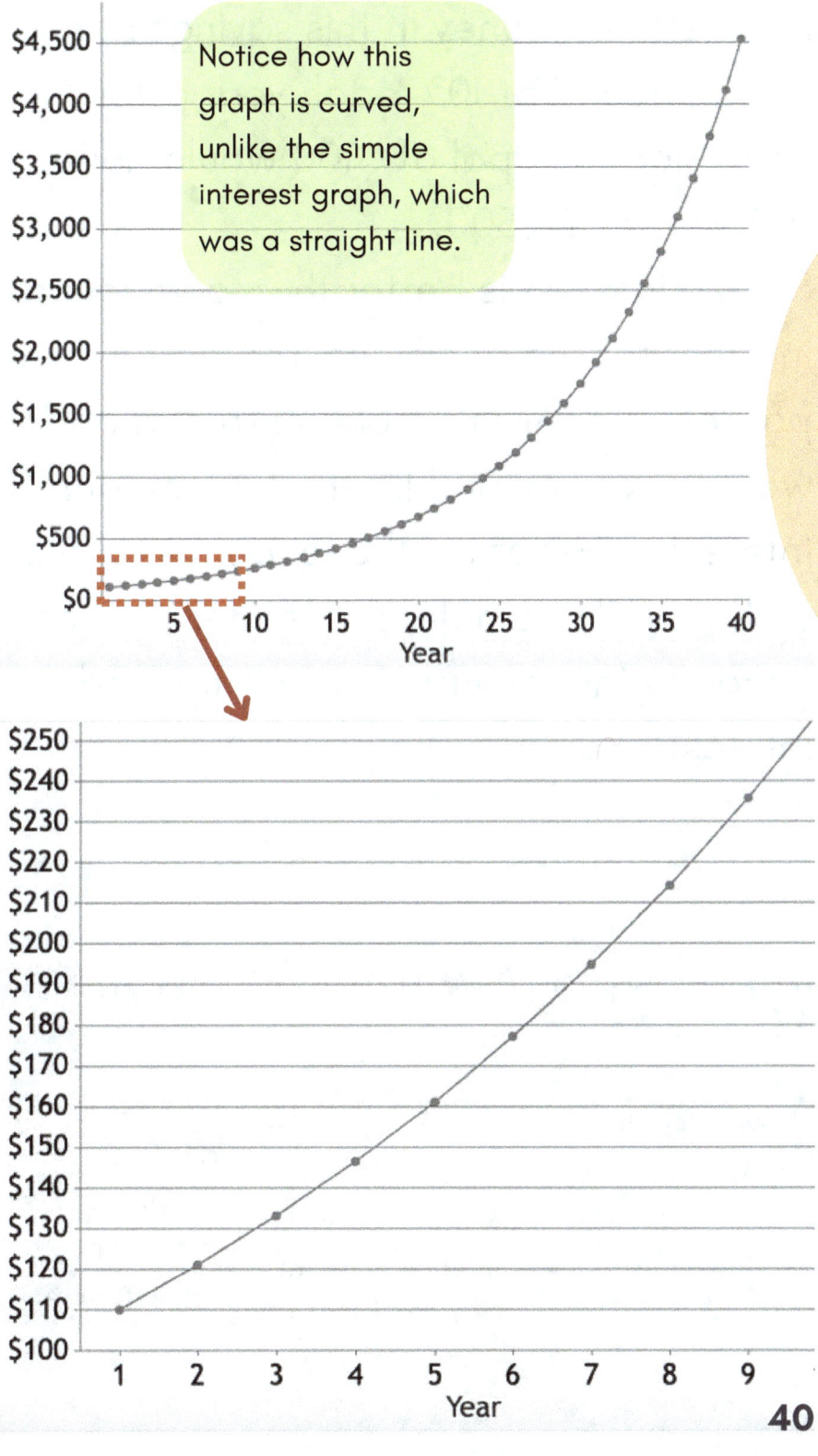

Notice how this graph is curved, unlike the simple interest graph, which was a straight line.

If Jill left her money in this savings account to compound at 10% each year after 40 years her principal of $100 would have turned into $4,500.

Simple interest is better than compound interest for the borrower. The borrower will pay less money in simple interest than they would in compound interest. Compound interest is better for the lender. As you saw with the Jill example, the lender can make exponential amounts from compound interest.

Compound Interest Formula

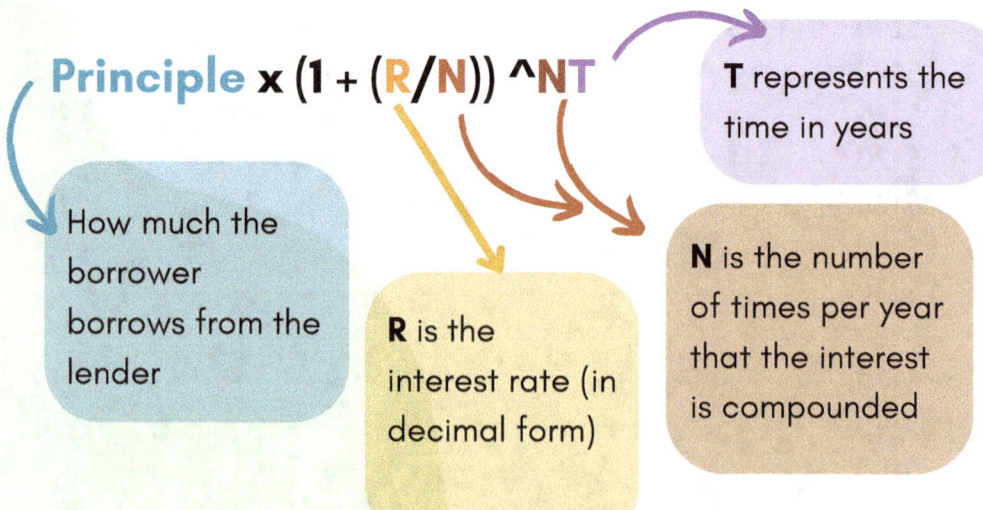

Principle x (1 + (R/N)) ^NT

T represents the time in years

How much the borrower borrows from the lender

R is the interest rate (in decimal form)

N is the number of times per year that the interest is compounded

When you are borrowing money, you want to find the lowest interest rate possible.

An Example

Let's say Jack wants to buy a car and he is looking for a car loan for $10,000. The first lender he goes to offers him a 5-year loan with 8% interest. Jack decides to go to a second lender who offers him a 5-year loan with only 7% interest. Jack should choose the 2nd loan because it has a lower interest rate. With the first loan, Jack would have ended up paying $12,166 ($2,166 of that is interest). But with the 2nd loan, Jack would end up paying only $11,880 ($1,880 of that is interest). As you can see, the 1% interest rate difference could have cost Jack $286. This is why it's important to do your research and look for loans with lower interest rates.

While you can't control interest rates completely, you can help bring down your interest rate by maintaining a high credit score.

Sometimes lenders will stretch out a loan over a long period of time. While the monthly payments are less, the overall amount you pay is more. In the example, if Jack took a loan that still had 7% interest, but was stretched out over 6 years (instead of 5 years) he would end up paying $2,275 in interest, which is $395 more than the 5-year loan at 7% interest, and $109 more then the 5-year loan at 8% interest.

When you are investing, it benefits you to find investments with higher interest rates. Think about the reverse of the Jack example, if you were looking out in the lender's best interest, not Jack's. If you were the lender you would want to charge the highest interest rate possible, so that you could make more money.

Chapter Review & Questions

- Interest is a percentage that the borrower pays to the lender for borrowing their money.
- The principle is the initial amount that is lent to a person or entity.
- Simple interest is better for the borrower because the interest payment is the same each time.
- Compound interest is better for the lender because the interest payments can increase dramatically.
- When graphed simple interest is a straight line and compound interest is a curved line

- Do you understand how interest works?
- Can you think of a time when you, a friend, or a family member used interest?
- Have you learned about interest in math class? What about your other classes?

Interest (and the formulas) can be difficult concepts at first. If they don't make sense that's okay. As you spend more time with finances, they will make sense eventually.

Chapter 7:
Investing

Investing can be a bit risky, but also a great way to make your money work for you. However, before you start investing it's important to make sure you know what you're doing.

Goals

Think about what your goals are with investing. Do you want short-term investments or long-term investments? Are you willing to risk more to potentially earn more? Do you just want to invest a little for fun, or do you want to make a significant amount of money from investing? These are all things you want to consider before you start investing.

Diversification and Risk

When investing there is always some amount of risk involved. It's important to consider what you can afford to lose. If you have a car payment and a phone bill that you have to pay each month, don't invest the money that you would use to make those payments (especially when you first start investing). Diversification is a great way to lower risk when investing. Diversification is when someone has many different investments. Have you ever heard the saying "Don't put all your eggs in one basket"? Well, that's what you should do with investing. Try not to only invest in 1 stock (for example).

Liquidity

Liquidity or something being liquid means that it's easy to get your money out of it. For example, a savings account would be very liquid because you can just withdraw your money. Typically the more liquid an investment is, the less interest it earns. A house would not be a liquid investment. It's a very long process to sell a house, and that could take months.

Why Invest?

Investing is a way to let your money work for you. If you go to an hourly job, you have to work for all the money you make. If you invest, you can buy an investment once and let the investment gather interest, meanwhile, you can be doing something else.

Passive income is regular earnings that you make without being actively involved in something. For example, if you get dividends from a stock, that would be considered passive income. Passive income allows you to earn money, and not have to work for it. For example, if you have $1,000 just sitting in a savings account, you could use it to buy a CD (which you'll learn about later). If you bought a $1,000, 2-year CD at 5% APY (annual percentage yield), at the end of 2 years you would make $102.50. In comparison, if you worked at a job making minimum wage ($7.25/hour), it would take a little over 14 hours of working to make that $102.50.

Passive income and investing can be very helpful to help you get financially ahead. While investing is an amazing concept that has many benefits, it's important to remember that there are some risks involved. In the example, CDs are a safe investment, but they are not liquid. Meaning if for some reason in those 2-years you needed to access that $1,000, you would have to pull it out of a CD and be penalized. This is by no means meant to discourage you from investing, it's just important to know what the risk is and if you are willing and able to take them.

Different Ways to Invest

CDs (Certificate of Deposit): A CD is a great, low-risk way for people to invest. A CD is a savings product that allows you to earn interest on a lump sum of money for a certain amount of time. Typically CDs are above $500 and if you withdraw money early you can lose interest and/or pay a penalty fee. CDs typically have more interest than a savings account and are very low risk. For example, Debbie could go to her bank and buy a CD for $1,900. The banker will show her the different CDs the bank offers. For example, they might have a CD with better interest and a longer period and another CD with a shorter period and lower interest. Debbie might decide to buy an 18-month CD with 5% APY (annual percentage yield). This means for the next 18 months Debbie can not use the $1,900 she put in the CD. After 18 months, Debbie would have a total of $2,044.27.

Mutual Funds: A mutual fund is a group of assets that invest in bonds, stocks, and other securities. Active manage mutual funds employ professional management teams to choose the assets that they invest in, in hopes of making as much money as possible. When an investor buys a mutual fund, they will typically end up paying a load and an expense ratio. The expense ratio is the rate the investor pays the manager of the fund (the people in charge of buying and selling the securities (assets) within the fund). The expense ratio is typically charged annually. The load is the amount paid to the financial advisor or broker. The broker is the person who sells the mutual fund to the investor (they kind of act like a salesperson). Sometimes they can offer advice on different funds and provide insight. The broker will typically charge this load at either the time of purchasing the mutual fund (front-end) or at the time of selling the mutual fund (back-end).

The 2 main types of mutual funds based on the objective of the fund are growth stock mutual funds (which typically have risky stocks in growing companies) and value stock mutual funds (which typically invest in stable companies). There are also mutual funds based on what securities the fund invests in. Equity mutual funds buy stocks, fixed-income mutual funds buy bonds, and balanced mutual funds buy both stocks and bonds. There are other types of mutual funds as well, these are just a few.

With mutual funds, there are also different share classes. 3 types of share classes are class A, B, and C shares. Class A shares have lower expense ratios and higher upfront fees (which are deducted from the initial investment). The upfront fees will typically be reduced for larger investments. Because Class A shares are front-loaded funds, they are typically the best type for long-term investments. Class B shares have higher expense ratios and high exit fees, but if they are held for a long time they can convert to class A shares. Class B shares have no upfront fee, but higher expense ratios. They can convert to A shares in 8 years, but you typically would have already spent more money in the higher expense ratios, so owning a Class B share isn't worth it. For this reason, they are pretty rare and uncommon. Class C shares have higher expense ratios than class A shares and lower than B shares, but they have a small exit fee that is waived usually after 1 year. They do not have front-end fees, so the entire initial investment earns interest income, and they have a small back-end load, that is usually removed once the shares have been held for over a year. Because class C shares don't convert into class A shares, they don't have the opportunity for lower expense ratios, meaning that as time increases, your investment returns will be reduced (due to the higher expense ratios). This makes them better for short-term investors. It's important to do research before investing in mutual funds. Mutual funds will typically have a prospectus. This is a document that provides the potential investor with all the information about the mutual fund including fees and minimum investment. Another good resource when considering mutual funds and ETFs is the Morningstar risk rating. This is a 1 to 5 point rating, where 5 is given to the best risk performers and 1 is given to the worst risk performers.

Hard Assets: Hard assets are items that increase in value over time. For example, while a regular car might lose value over time, a nice classic car may gain value. Or a nice piece of artwork may be constantly gaining value as time goes on. Some common hard assets include real estate, gold, oil, and other commodities.

Bonds: A bond is a certificate issued by a public company or the government stating that they will repay you the money you invest in a certain period of time at a certain interest rate. For example, let's say Carol starts an oil company. The oil company does great so she decides to expand but she doesn't have enough money to expand. Carol might decide to issue bonds. Carol decides that each bond is a loan for $1,000 (principal), which she will pay back to the investor in 5 years (maturity date). To make it worthwhile for the investor, each bond also pays a 5% interest rate (this is known as a coupon rate when using bonds) each year. Suzy has a lot of savings and is looking to invest some of her extra cash. She decides to buy one of Carol's oil company's bonds. Suzy pays $1,000 for the bond, and for the next 5 years, she gets $50 in interest each year. At the end of the 5 years, Carol pays Suzy (and the other investors) back the original $1,000. This works well for both Suzy and Carol. Carol's oil company got the money it needed to expand and Suzy got to make an extra $250, just by buying a bond. Bonds are typically considered less risky than stocks, but this doesn't mean they're risk-free. One risk investors face is the issuer (Carol's oil company in the example) may default on paying back the principal. This means that if Carol's oil company hadn't expanded successfully, they may not have been able to pay back Suzy and the other investors their $1,000. Bonds with higher coupon rates are more risky. Along with that government bonds are normally considered more stable than corporate bonds. It's important to do research on the issuer before buying a bond.

Stocks: When you buy a stock, you are purchasing a share (a small piece of that company); this represents fractional ownership in a company. Some stocks issue dividends, but with other stocks, shareholders make money by selling stocks. The goal with stocks is quite simple: buy low, sell high. This, however, is easier said than done. A person will normally buy a stock in a company if they think that company will do well (thus the stock will go up in value). Public companies can sell their stocks through a stock market exchange, and people looking to invest can buy or sell their stocks through a stockbroker. A company might sell shares of their company if they need money to expand or pay off debt. If you think a company will do well, you might buy 5 shares at $80 each (so you would pay $400 total). Let's say 3 months later, that same company's stock price increases to $90 a share. You could decide to sell, and you would end up selling the 5 shares for a total of $450, meaning that you would make $50. Beware that companies can decrease in price too, meaning that you might lose money. That's why diversification is important. Another way shareholders can make money is through dividends. Some stocks will pay dividends, which is a regular payment to shareholders, typically quarterly. Not all stocks pay dividends, only certain ones do.

An example of a dividend would be a stock that pays $0.15 per share a quarter. If someone owned 100 shares of that stock they could make $45 a year, just from buying stocks. It's important to keep in mind that companies can change how much and if they issue dividends. Dividends are based on a company's willingness and are not consistent. If you purchase a stock that issues $0.15 a quarter, but then the company decides to only pay $0.05 a quarter in dividends, some of the shareholders may sell the stock, and cause the stock price to drop.

ETFs (Exchange Traded Funds): ETFs are a basket of different securities that trade similarly to a stock. Because an ETF can include a variety of different investments (like stocks and bonds), they are very diversified. ETFs are traded on a stock exchange, so they are bought and sold like stocks. This means that ETFs are liquid and an ETF can be bought and sold multiple times in a day and they are traded by a secondary market (unlike mutual funds, which are traded once per day by the fund company). When someone buys an ETF, they have to pay commission and other related fees. Management fees, however, are typically lower for an ETF than for a mutual fund, because typically ETFs are not actively managed. Different ETFs have different objectives. Some are meant to be an overall market index, meaning that they represent what the market is doing overall (kind of like the S&P 500). Other ETFs track the performance of certain sectors. For example, an ETF might have securities from only the technology sector, meaning that if one day the technology sector increases in general, so might the ETF.

ETFs have different objectives and offer different amounts of diversification. Specific sector ETFs typically provide less diversification than ETFs that try to replicate an index. An investor can make money through an ETF by the ETF rising in its market price and/or the investor can make money through dividends. Similar to stocks, if the securities within an ETF stock price rise, so will the ETF. This means that an investor could buy an ETF and then once the price rises, sell it for that higher price. The investor would have made money from the difference in price. It's important to remember that the ETF price could decrease too. Meaning that if the investor bought an ETF at a higher price than what they sold it at, they would lose money. Like stocks, some ETFs issue dividends. An investor could receive dividends from their ETF if the ETF chooses to issue dividends. Some ETFs will not issue dividends and will instead put the money back into investing for that ETF. Let's say that you are looking to buy an investment that will add diversification to your portfolio. After doing research, and looking at a variety of ETFs, you find an ETF that fits your objectives. You could then purchase the ETF through a broker (like you would a stock). This means that you only had to purchase one ETF, but still have the diversification of multiple securities. By doing this, you were able to save time on research and analysis. ETFs typically require a low minimum investment because you can just buy one share (plus commission and fees). Overall, ETFs can provide diversification to an investor's portfolio (like a mutual fund) while having the liquidity of stocks.

Index Fund: Index funds are funds that track a market index. Some examples of index funds are index mutual funds and index ETFs. Typically index funds deliver returns that are similar to an index of investments like the S&P 500. They are built to have a similar performance to a major market index. Because they track so many different investments, they are typically very diversified. Index funds typically deliver slightly lower returns than an index because of the fees that are associated with them. However, index funds typically have fewer expenses than an actively managed fund. In other words, when a fund is actively managed (securities within the fund are being sold and bought often) there are typically more fees. But with index funds that are not actively managed, there tend to be fewer fees, which can lead to a big difference in the money made from the investment over a long period of time. Index funds can increase in value, which would benefit the investor, but they can also decrease in value, which would not benefit the investor. As with all investments, it's important to do research before purchasing an investment.

Chapter Review & Questions

- Consider your investment goals before you start investing.
- Liquidity is how easy it is to get your money out of an investment.
- It's important to diversify your investments (Don't only invest in one thing).
- A CD (certificate of deposit) allows you to earn interest on a lump sum of money over a specified amount of time. They are low-risk and not liquid.
- A bond is a certificate issued by a public company or the government stating that they will repay you money at a certain time at a certain interest rate.
- A mutual fund is a group of assets that invest in bonds, stocks, and other securities.
- When you buy a stock you are buying a share of a company.
- Hard assets are physical things you own that you can get money out of.

- Does investing interest you?
- When investing are you looking for less risk or are you fine risking a little?
- Do you want long-term or short-term investments?
- Do you currently own any investments?

Chapter 8:

Ways to Make Money

While reading this book you have learned how to save, budget, and invest your money, but how can you make money in the first place? Here are some ideas:

Start Your Own Business: This is not a simple way to make money, but if you are creative or an entrepreneur at heart, this can be a great way to make money. You will most likely need your parent's help, but you can make a product and sell it at farmer's markets or online (like Etsy, for example). You could also do a service like mowing lawns.

Get A Job: You want to make sure that it's legal in your state to work at your age, but if it is legal, working somewhere can teach you lots of valuable skills. Ask your parents or other adults for suggestions on where to work, or if you already have a place in mind, reach out to that company and see if they are hiring.

Babysitting: If you like children this could be the perfect job for you. You could ask neighbors with young kids if they need a babysitter or use a trustworthy website to find babysitting jobs near you! You could also take a free or paid babysitting course to become a certified babysitter.

Tutor Kids: Are you great at a subject or do you like teaching others? Tutoring kids can help you earn a little extra cash. Even if you aren't great at a subject, you can still help children that are younger than you learn a concept. Reach out to your school and see if they need tutors. You could even teach kids a non-academic skill, like learning an instrument.

Odd Jobs: See if neighbors or your parents have any odd jobs that need to be done. This might be raking leaves in the fall, planting flowers, weeding, cleaning, packing, etc.

Freelance: There are lots of freelance websites online where you can put your writing or creative skills to use. Some magazines even allow teens to write a section monthly! If you like making videos, you could even start a YouTube channel. There are so many ways to make money online, and all you have to do is search. One thing to remember is to be careful of scams and only use trustworthy websites. If you are unsure, ask your parents or a trusted adult to get their opinion, it's better to be safe than sorry.

Investing: This is a risky way to make money, but if you are successful, it can allow you to make money easily. Even if you only have a small amount of money you could start investing through some of the different ways discussed in the Investing chapter of this book.

Be creative! These were just a few simple ideas for things you could do. Do you have the next great invention? Turn that into a way to make money. Think about what you are passionate about, and see how you could make money from doing that. Whatever it is, think outside the box and you're sure to come up with something.

Chapter Review & Questions

- What are some ways you would like to make money?

_____

_____

_____

_____

_____

_____

_____

_____

Chapter 9:
Inflation

Do you ever hear people complaining about how much gas prices have gone up? Do people ever say how much cheaper something was 20 years ago? Inflation is the rate at which prices increase over a certain time. Inflation represents how much more expensive a good or service is. Look at the graphic below to see how much coffee prices have increased between 1970 and 2022 (according to Investopedia).

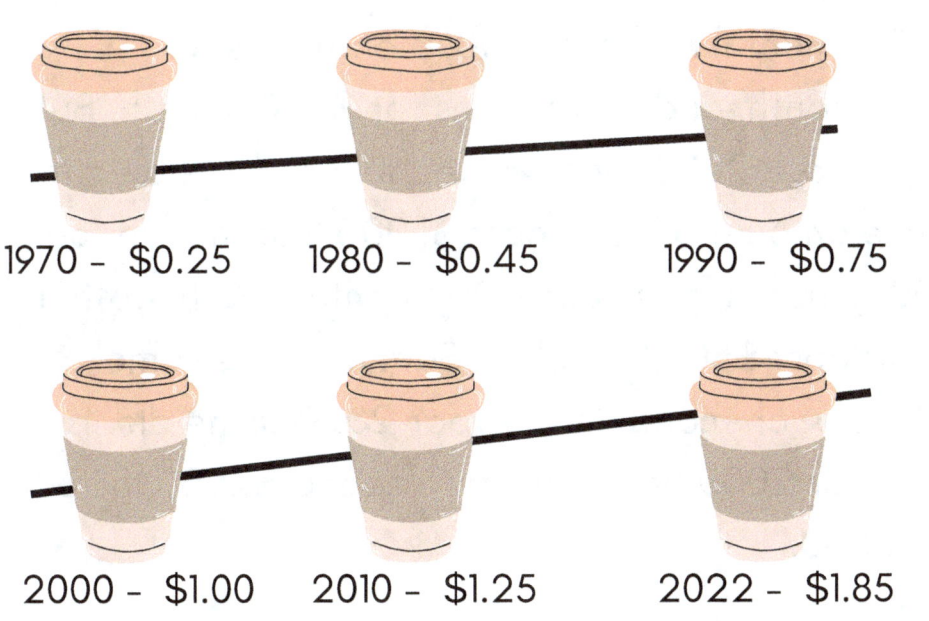

1970 – $0.25   1980 – $0.45   1990 – $0.75

2000 – $1.00   2010 – $1.25   2022 – $1.85

Why did the coffee increase by $1.60? The coffee didn't change. There was nothing more special about the coffee made in 2022 than the coffee made in 1970. The coffee increased in price due to inflation. Inflation is common in an economy. If someone's income does not increase as much as inflation, then they are worse off, because they can't buy as much.

An example:

Let's say in the year 2000 Sam made $1,000 a month and with that, he bought food for $500/month, rent for $300/month, gas for $50/month, and other items for $250/month. But in the year 2020, Sam makes $1,500, but now the same amount of food cost $1,000/month, rent cost $600/month, gas cost $100/month, and the other items cost $500/month. If Sam buys the same things each month in the year 2020 as he did in the year 2000 he will have to spend $2000 instead of $1000.

If Sam's income increased with inflation (200% over 20 years), he wouldn't have a problem, but because Sam's income only increased by $500 instead of $1000, he can't buy all the things he used to be able to buy. This is an example of how inflation could cause problems.

Note: The numbers used in the example are for simplicity and understanding purposes only.

Imagine you are saving for retirement and how difficult it would be with inflation. If in 2000 Sam planned on saving $1000/year for retirement, by 2020 it would cost him twice as much. So does that mean someone just has to save a lot more than they think they need? Not exactly. Typically by investing money, people are able to counteract inflation.

According to Worlddata.info, between 1960 and 2022 the average inflation rate was 3.8% a year. This means if you can find an investment with an interest rate higher than the average inflation rate, you can protect your money against inflation. It's important to remember that you don't want to keep your savings in risky investments. Make sure where you invest your money is safe, and if it is risky, you can afford to lose however much you invest.

Inflation isn't something to be scared of or dread dealing with. When you understand inflation and how it works, you can get ahead of it and be financially secure.

Chapter Review & Questions

- Inflation is the rate at which prices increase over a certain time.
- By investing you can counteract inflation.
- Inflation is something to accept, and not be scared of or dread.

- Have you ever experienced inflation?
- What's something that you have noticed an increase in price?
- Have you heard adults talking about how expensive prices are now?

Start paying attention to prices and see if you can spot inflation!

Conclusion

Now that you know the basics of money management, start managing your money wisely. Whether that's spending less on wants, opening a savings account, or even investing, I encourage you to start somewhere. If you still feel lost on where to start, think about what you want in the future (sometimes it helps to work backward). Create goals depending on that. Maybe you want to get a car or have a certain amount of money saved by the time you are a certain age, whatever it is, write a goal, come up with a plan, and stick to it. If you don't already have an emergency fund, you should start saving and putting that money into an emergency fund. I also suggest that you open a savings account if you haven't already. Savings accounts help you save money and not spend it. Depending on what your finances look like, I think putting spare money in a low-risk investment is a great idea. Use the next few pages of the book to start planning your financial future.

Smart Goal #1:

_____

_____

_____

_____

I will achieve this goal by doing...

_____

_____

_____

Steps I need to take to achieve this goal:

☐ _____

☐ _____

☐ _____

☐ _____

Smart Goal #2:

_____

_____

_____

_____

I will achieve this goal by doing...

_____

_____

_____

Steps I need to take to achieve this goal:

☐ _____

☐ _____

☐ _____

☐ _____

Do you have a $400 emergency fund?

NO   **YES**

That's okay, let's
make a plan!

Great Job!

What can I do to make money?

_____

_____

How will I make sure I don't spend the money I make?

_____

_____

Here's a chart you can fill out as you save money to put into your emergency fund.

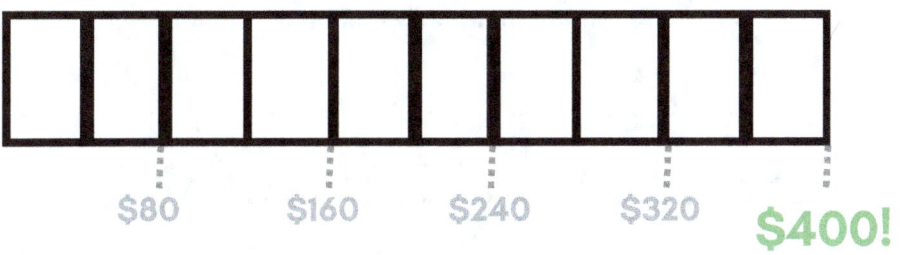

$80 $160 $240 $320

$400!

My Savings Log!

Fill in the squares with different progressions of numbers depending on how much you want to save. If you think you can save a lot, write bigger numbers, but if you don't think you can save as much, write smaller numbers. If you already have savings, put the amount you have saved at the bottom of the piggy bank. As you save, color in the piggy bank!

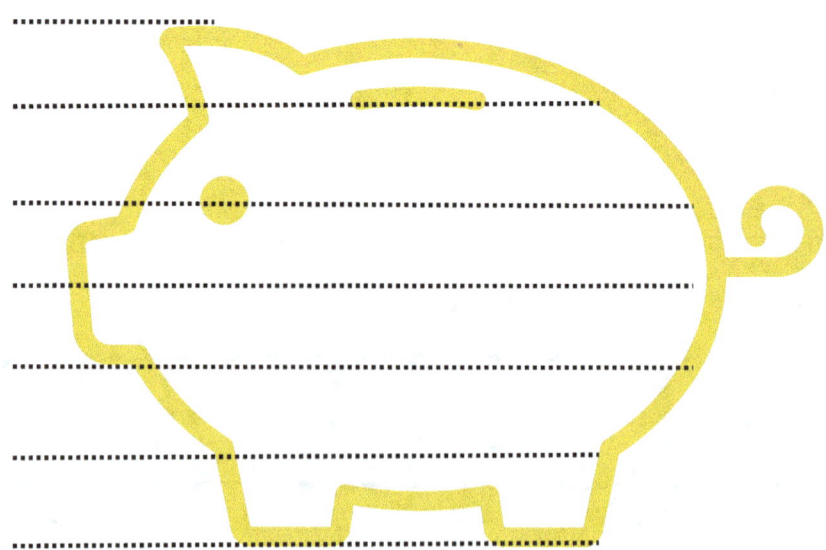

Try creating a budget!

For the next month write down your expenses on this page and your income (any time you get money) on the next page.

What I Spent Money On: The Amount:

How I Made Money:	The Amount:

Look back on your expenses and on your income for the last month. Did you spend more than you made? Is that what you thought you spent your money on? See how much money you spent on needs and how much you spent on wants. Try to see if you could spend less money in one category and put more money into savings. Look at your income and see what jobs paid the most money. Think about what jobs you liked the most. Try using what you learned in Chapter 3 to create a budget of your own!

If you enjoyed reading this, please leave a review on Amazon! I read every review and they help new readers discover my books.

Vocabulary

APY (Annual Percentage Yield): The amount of interest or money that you earn over one year.

Asset: Something that holds value.

Bond: A security where the issuer owes the holder money and typically pays interest. See page 54.

Borrower: A person who borrows money from a lender. See page 35.

Budget: An estimated income and plan for how to spend income. See page 22.

CD (Certificate of Deposit): A certificate issued to a person depositing money for a specific amount of time. See page 49.

Closed-end Credit: Credit or a loan that is only for a specified amount of money (typically for an item) for a specified amount of time. Example: car loan. See page 29.

Compound Interest: Interest that is added to the principal sum; interest on interest. See page 38.

Credit: An arrangement to pay later for something. See page 28.

Credit Score (FICO Score): A number representing a person's creditworthiness. See page 30.

Debt: An obligation that requires one person to pay money to another. See page 35.

Diversification: When a portfolio has many different types of investments. See page 46.

Dividends: A sum of money that is regularly paid to shareholders.

Emergency Fund: An allotted amount of money that is saved to be used on emergencies only. See page 13.

ETF (Exchange Traded Fund): A basket of different securities that trade similarly to a stock. See page 58.

Expense: The cost of something; how much something costs.

FICO Score (Credit Score): A number representing a person's creditworthiness. See page 30.

Finances: The management of money.

Fixed Expense: An expense where the amount doesn't change. See page 23.

Hard Asset: A physical item that holds value. See page 53.

Income: Money received through work or investments.

Inflation: A general increase in prices and a decrease in purchasing power. See page 68.

Interest: Money paid regularly at a specific rate as a cost to borrow money. See page 35.

Investing: Spending money or buying an asset with the hopes of gaining money from it. See page 45.

Lender: A person who lets a borrower borrow money from them. See page 35.

Line of Credit: A borrowing limit that can be used at any time.

Liquid (Liquidity): How easy it is to sell an asset or get your money out of an investment. See page 46.

Loan: Money that is borrowed and expected to pay back.

Loan Sharks: People who give out bad loans. See page 33.

Long-term Investment: An investment that is kept for typically over 5 years.

Mutual Fund: A fund that pools money and is professionally managed. See page 50.

Needs vs. Wants: Items that are necessary vs. items that are nice or ideal, but not necessary. See page 14.

Open-End Credit: A loan that the borrower can use money repeatedly. Ex: Credit Card. See page 29.

Passive Income: Regular earnings that one doesn't have to actively work for. See page 47.

Principle: The initial amount invested.

Savings Account: An low-risk and low-interest account that is a safe place for people to keep their money. See page 18.

Shareholder: A person who owns a share(s).

Short-term Investment: An investment that is kept for typically less than 3 years.

Simple Interest: Interest rate paid based on the principle of the loan (interest is not added to the principal amount). See page 36.

Smart Goals: A system for goal setting. See page 6.

Stocks: The shares of which ownership of a corporation is divided. See page 55.

Variable Expenses: Expenses in which the amount changes. See page 23.

Withdraw: When a person takes money out of something (typically a bank account).

Acknowledgments

Writing a book can be difficult and I wouldn't have been able to do it without the help of these incredible people:
I would like to thank my amazing and thoughtful family for their love and support. They have given me so much encouragement, advice, and wisdom. I would like to thank my teachers and other financial professionals who have taught me a great deal about finance. Above all, I thank God and Jesus for their mercy and everything that they have done in my life.

About the Author

Serena Allen is an entrepreneur and business owner. She has a passion for finance and she intends on getting a degree in business or economics. Serena has taken many finance, business, and economics classes and strives to increase financial literacy across American youth. Diving into Finance is the first book Serena has written, but she hopes to write more books in the future.